THREE IRISH PLAYS

THE LAND OF HEART'S DESIRE
By WILLIAM BUTLER YEATS

THE TWISTING OF THE ROPE
By DOUGLAS HYDE

RIDERS TO THE SEA
By J. M. SYNGE

With An Introduction By
Harrison Hale Schaff

BOSTON

INTERNATIONAL POCKET LIBRARY

Branden Books, Boston

ISBN 9780828314572 Paperback
ISBN 9780828325691 E-Book

International Pocket Library
division of,
Branden Books

www.brandenbooks.com

Three Irish Plays

INTRODUCTION

That the Irish Literary Renaissance is best known and most highly regarded by reason of its contribution to dramatic literature is an almost universal judgment, though drama by no means monopolized the activity of that movement, neither was it in the world of letters, nor the theatre, that this renaissance played its most important part.

Its real accomplishment is its contribution to the evidence in support of the claim of Irish nationality.

When the Powers met at Versailles at the conclusion of the World War to formulate a treaty of peace and once again to make over the map of a substantial part of Europe, they were confronted with the necessity of considering the insistent demands of a number of claimants seeking recognition and the status of independent autonomous nations. All of these claimants had long since lost their political independence and been incorporated in alien governments—even their names, in some cases, were hardly remembered save in the European chancellories.

While political expediency, geographical features as related to military operations, and economic considerations, played an important part in the final determinations at Versailles, "the right of self determination" as formulated by Mr. Wilson and accorded to each of the successful groups of claimants, was based on a formula of the following nature:

That the claimant group had a continuous national consciousness, that is, a conviction of their own homogeneity as a group distinct in its aspirations for self government from any alien or related group. That historically the claimant had enjoyed independence of which it had been deprived by *force majeure*, that the culture of the original nation during its period of autonomous existence had persisted in its essential characteristics down to the present time and not been so merged in the culture of the country of which it was nominally a part as to lose its identity and individuality. An example of such mingling being the absorption of the Scandinavian Normans by the French while on the other hand Poland, notwithstanding her three partitions and the constant coercion of her conquerors, retained her national consciousness and cultural aspects.

Different as is the understanding among scholars and statesmen of what constitutes a complete definition of national culture there is a substantial agreement that the spoken and written languages of a people, its religion, art, literature, social customs, traditional history, and folk lore, each are constituent factors which, coupled with their continued maintenance and a continuously expressed consciousness of nationality, qualifies the group so constituted to the right of self determining their political future, in so far as the cultural requirement goes.

After the fabrication of the Treaty of Versailles it was self evident that a reconsideration of the claims of Irish nationality would have to be entertained by the English government and decided in principle at least in conformity with the enlightened opinion of the world based on the accepted conditions precedent to the right of self determination.

No influence contributed more to preparing the mind of the English people to an acknowledgment of the maintenance of the distinct and individual culture of Ireland in the field of language, tradition, and literature than the accomplishments and activities of the Irish Literary Renaissance. It rounded out with indisputable proof that part of the Versailles formula for self determination incident to the broad and varied cultural field in which it labored.

While it was at the very close of the nineteenth century that the Literary Renaissance in Ireland first attracted any general attention abroad and the first decade of the twentieth century in which the movement established its unquestionable place in world literature was yet to come, it, like all such movements, had its beginning in earlier years.

The Eighteen Eighties, as is well known, marked the inception of the Continental and English revolt against the attenuated, devitalized, primly formalized literary product of the Victorian School, and culminated in the then sensational and in many respects brilliant era of the Nineties. The Irish Literary Renaissance started at approximately the same time, and while its writers, scholars, and teachers no doubt were conscious of the low level to which creative literature had fallen in England, on the Continent, and for that matter throughout the world, they held, as is characteristic of their race, a special brief for their literary revolt and sought a quite different verdict than their coeval workers in other countries, who aspired only to the revitalizing of literature in terms and symbols of the revalued values of their age.

Like all special briefs that of the Irish Literary Renaissance was complex. It indicted the novels of the popular and pecuniarily successful Charles Lever as travesties on Irish character, a distortion of Irish history, a slander on Irish society which combined in presenting to the public an entirely erroneous picture of Ireland and everything really Irish. To this disservice they added that of Dion Boucicault, whose plays and characters they charged created drama reflecting the concepts of those novelists and merely transferred to the boards the stage Irishmen of the novels, to parade once again and revive their untruths before a public that had begun to lose sight of the earlier novels.

In like manner it rejected as unrelated to Ireland in its historical, cultural, and emotional aspects the work of a large group of brilliant, Irish born authors, charging that it was essentially English literature, a contention that is sustained on any careful critical analysis.

Had the Renaissance merely been interested in discrediting the work of these and kindred authors, it would have been fighting windmills. Its motivation was deeper than that and far more purposeful. It resorted neither to elaborate critical condemnations nor invective. It sought rather to present for the judgment of the world a native literature that would reflect the deep underlying emotions, aspirations, and culture of Ireland, fused into a composite of truth and beauty.

That such a program had a background of racial and national consciousness and pride needs no argument, nor was the effort to generalize the use of Gaelic speech and writing attributable to any motive unrelated to such a background. Of political aims and agitation the Renaissance was quite innocent. That was a field which through the centuries had never lain fallow but ever echoed with claims of nationality and demands for freedom—a field often drenched in blood and one from which many a man had been snatched to adorn a gibbet. In the days of the Renaissance it was as crowded as ever, for to such activities the Irish genius beckons far more than to the field of letters and scholarly endeavor. The Renaissance had its own work to do and did it well, supplementing, justifying and in a decisive manner contributing to the ultimate success of those aspirations Ireland has so long treasured and for which she had sacrificed so much.

Another divergence of the Irish Literary Renaissance from the contemporary movement elsewhere was that its program chiefly concerned itself with exploiting the classic Gaelic literature of Ireland, and drawing on that source, so rich in history, tradition, and folklore, for themes to be represented by modern authors while on the other hand Continental and English authors were seeking only to forget the literary past in an incessant striving for creations original in both form and substance.

Fine as much of the scholarship was that devoted itself to the classics, tuneful and imaginative as were the poets, faithful to the lore of their race as were the prose writers, it was the dramatic writers who most impressively evidenced the continuity of and still vital influence of the ancient and distinct racial culture of Ireland in the lives of the mass of the contemporary people.

If objection be raised that the drama of this movement in its outstanding and most influential products was a peasant drama, it should be remembered that the great bulk of Irish population is of that class, tilling the soil or wresting a living from the sea; and that not only in Ireland but throughout the world, it is in that class or analogous classes, least touched by alien influences, that the true culture of a race or nation is to be found.

Of this little book so far nothing has been said, and very little will be said. This introduction aims not to epitomize the three representative plays of the Irish Literary Renaissance it contains but to suggest to the reader the rationalization of their existence and their correlation to one of those great resurgent movements which marks the evolution of social and political history.

William Butler Yeats, the most conspicuous member of a talented family, is rightly regarded as the greatest single influence in the Irish Literary Renaissance. A number of his fellow authors matched in merit his literary productions, and one at least decisively surpassed him, but his was the first success. Freely he lent his prestige to the movement, wise counsel and encouragement to struggling authors, and kept a guiding hand on the rudder in the early days and stormy waters through which the dramatic movement had to navigate. He is represented in this volume by *The Land of Heart's Desire.*

The Twisting of the Rope by Douglas Hyde is the author's English version of his play written in Gaelic. It was produced at Dublin in 1901 in Gaelic as a part of the program of the concluding performances of the Irish National Theatre, founded by Edward Martyn, which was succeeded by the well known Abbey Theatre group. It has the distinction of being the first play performed in the Gaelic language.

John M. Synge, by far the outstanding dramatist of the Renaissance, whose futile efforts in the field of French literary criticism Yeats happily was able to persuade him to abandon in favor of a sojourn on the western islands off the Bay of Galloway for the purpose of imbuing Synge with the realization of the survival of primitive Irish culture, and which resulted in his famous "Aran Islands," illustrated by Jack Yeats, is here represented by his masterpiece, *Riders to the Sea.*

This play, universally acclaimed, was shortly after its appearance hailed by English critics as the finest example of dramatic tragedy produced since the Elizabethan era, a critical judgment that to this day has passed unchallenged.

HARRISON HALE SCHAFF

THE LAND OF HEART'S DESIRE

BY WILLIAM BUTLER YEATS

TO
FLORENCE FARR

O Rose, thou art sick.

WILLIAM BLAKE

PERSONS OF THE PLAY

MAURTEEN   BRUIN.
BRIDGET BRUIN.
SHAWN BRUIN.
MARY BRUIN.
FATHER HART.
A FAERY CHILD.

*The Scene is laid in the Barony of Kilmacowen, in
the County of Sligo, and at a remote time.*

SCENE—*A room with a hearth, on the floor in the middle of a deep alcove to the right. There are benches in the alcove and a table; and a crucifix on the wall. The alcove is full of a glow of light from the fire. There is an open door facing the audience to the left, and to the left of this a bench. Through the door one can see the forest. It is night, but the moon or a late sunset glimmers through the trees and carries the eye far off into a vague, mysterious world, Murteen Bruin, Shawn Bruin, and Bridgett Bruin sit in the alcove at the table or about the fire. They are dressed in the costume of some remote time, and near them sits an old priest,* FATHER HART. *He may be dressed as a friar. There is food and drink upon the table,* MARY BRUIN *stands by the door reading a book. If she looks up she can see through the door into the wood.*

BRIDGET.

Because I bid her clean the pots for supper She took
that old book down out of the thatch; She has been
doubled over it ever since. We should be deafened
by her groans and moans Had she to work as some
do, Father Hart; Get up at dawn like me and mend
and scour Or ride abroad in the boisterous night like
you, The pyx and blessed bread under your arm.

SHAWN.

Mother, you are too cross.

BRIDGET.

You've married **her,** And fear
to vex her and so take her part.

13

MAURTEEN *[to* FATHER HART].
It is but right that youth should side with youth;
She quarrels with my wife a bit at times,
And is too deep just now in the old book!
But do not blame her greatly; she will grow
As quiet as a puff-ball in a tree
When but the moons of marriage dawn and die
For half a score of times.

FATHER HART.
Their hearts are wild,
As be the hearts of birds, till children come.

BRIDGET.
She would not mind the kettle, milk the cow,
Or even lay the knives and spread the cloth.

SHAWN.
Mother, if only--

MAURTEEN.
Shawn, this is half empty;
Go, bring up the best bottle that we have.

FATHER HART.
I *never* saw her read a book before,
What can it be?

MAURTEEN *[to* SHAWN] .
What are you waiting for?
You must not shake it when you draw the cork;
It's precious wine, so take your time about it.
[To Priest.]   [SHAWN *goes.]*
There was a Spaniard wrecked at Ocris Head,
When I was young, and I have still some bottles.
He cannot bear to hear her blamed; the book
Has lain up in the thatch these fifty years;
My father told me my grandfather wrote it,

And killed a heifer for the binding of it
But supper's spread, and we can talk and eat.
It was little good he got out of the book,
Because it filled his house with rambling fidlers,
And rambling ballad-makers and the like.
The griddle-bread is there in front of you.
Colleen, what is the wonder in that book,
That you must leave the bread to cool?   Had I
Or had my father read or written books
There were no stocking stuffed with yellow guineas
To come when I am dead to Shawn and you.

FATHER HART.
You should not fill your head with foolish dreams.
What are you reading?

MARY.
How a Princess Edane,
A daughter of a King of Ireland, heard
A voice singing on a May Eve like this,
And followed half awake and half asleep,
Until she came into the Land of Faery,
Where nobody gets old and godly and grave,
Where nobody gets old and crafty and wise,
Where nobody gets old and bitter of tongue.
And she is still there, busied with a dance
Deep in the dewy shadow of a wood,
Or where stars walk upon a mountain-top.

MAURTEEN.
Persuade the colleen to put down the book;
My grandfather would mutter just such things,
And he was no judge of a dog or a horse,
And any idle boy could blarney him;
Just speak your mind.

FATHER HART.

           Put it away, my colleen; God
spreads the heavens above us like great wings
And gives a little round of deeds and days,
And then come the wrecked angels and set snares,
And bait them with light hopes and heavy dreams,
Until the heart is puffed with pride and goes
Half shuddering and half joyous from God's peace;
For it was some wrecked angel, blind with tears,
Who flattered Edane's heart with merry words.
My colleen, I have seen some other girls
Restless and ill at ease, but years went by
And they grew like their neighbours and were glad
In minding children, working at the churn,
And gossiping of weddings and of wakes;
For life moves out of a red flare of dreams
Into a common light of common hours,
Until old age brings the red flare again.

MAURTEEN.

That's true—but she's too young to know it's true.

BRIDGET.

She's old enough to know that it is wrong
To mope and idle.

MAURTEEN.

           I've little blame for her;
She's dull when my big son is in the fields,
And that and maybe this good woman's tongue
Have driven her to hide among her dreams
Like children from the dark under the bedclothes.

BRIDGET.

She'd never do a turn if I were silent.

MAURTEEN.

And maybe it is natural upon May Eve

To dream of the good people. But tell me, girl, If
you've the branch of blessed quicken wood That
women hang upon the post of the door That they
may send good luck into the house? Remember
they may steal new-married brides After the fall of
twilight on May Eve,
Or what old women mutter at the fire Is but a pack
of lies.

FATHER HART.
It may be truth.
We do not know the limit of those powers
God has permitted to the evil spirits
For some mysterious end. You have done right *[to* MARY] ;
It's well to keep old innocent customs up.

(MARY BRUIN *has taken a bough of quicken wood from a
seat and hung it on a nail in the door-post. A girl child
strangely dressed, perhaps in faery green, comes out of the
wood and takes it away.)*

MARY.
I had no sooner hung it on the nail
Before a child ran up out of the wind;
She has caught it in her hand and fondled it;
Her face is pale as water before dawn.

FATHER HART.
Whose child can this be?

MAURTEEN.
No one's child at all.
She often dreams that some one has gone by,
When there was nothing but a puff of wind.

MARY.
They have taken away the blessed quicken wood,
They will not bring good luck into the house;
Yet I am glad that I was courteous to them,

For are not they, likewise, children of God?

FATHER HART.

Colleen, they are the children of the fiend,
And they have power until the end of Time,
When God shall fight with them a great pitched battle
And hack them into pieces.

MARY.

He will smile,
Father, perhaps, and open His great door.

FATHER HART.

Did but the lawless angels see that door
They would fall, slain by everlasting peace;
And when such angels knock upon our doors,
Who goes with them must drive through the same storm.

*(An arm comes around the door-post and knocks and beck-
ons. It is clearly seen in the silvery light,* MARY BRUIN *goes to
door and stands in it for a moment,* MAURTEEN BRUIN *is busy
filling* FATHER HART'S *plate.* BRIDGET BRUIN *stirs the fire.)*

MARY *[coming to table].*

There's somebody out there that beckoned me
And raised her hand as though it held a cup,
And she was drinking from it, so it may be
That she is thirsty.

[She takes milk from the table and carries it to the door.]

FATHER HART.

That will be the child

That you would have it was no child at all.

BRIDGET.

And maybe, Father, what he said was true;
For there is not another night in the year
So wicked as to-night.

MAURTEEN.
Nothing can harm us
While the good Father's underneath our roof.

MARY.

A little queer old woman dressed in green.

BRIDGET.
The good people beg for milk and fire
Upon May Eve—woe to the house that gives,
For they have power upon it for a year.
MAURTEEN.
Hush, woman, hush!
BRIDGET.
She's given milk away.
I knew she would bring evil on the house.
MAURTEEN.
Who was it?
MARY.
Both the tongue and face were strange.

MAURTEEN.
Some strangers came last week to Clover Hill;
She must be one of them.
BRDDGET.
I am afraid.

FATHER HART.
The Cross will keep all evil from the house
While it hangs there.
MAURTEEN.
Come, sit beside me, colleen,
And put away your dreams of discontent,
For I would have you light up my last days,
Like the good glow of the turf; and when I die

You'll be the wealthiest hereabout, for, colleen,
I have a stocking full of yellow guineas
Hidden away where nobody can find it.

BRIDGET.

You are the fool of every pretty face,
And I must spare and pinch that my son's wife
May have all kinds of ribbons for her head.

MAURTEEN.

Do not be cross; she is a right good girl!
The butter is by your elbow, Father Hart.
My colleen, have not Fate and Time and Change
Done well for me and for old Bridget there?
We have a hundred acres of good land,
And sit beside each other at the fire.
I have this reverend Father for my friend,
I look upon your face and my son's face—
We've put his plate by yours—and here he comes,
And brings with him the only thing we have lacked,
Abundance of good wine [SHAWN *comes in*].
Stir up the fire,
And put new turf upon it till it blaze;
To watch the turf-smoke coiling from the fire,
And feel content and wisdom in your heart,
This is the best of life; when we are young
We long to tread a way none trod before,
But find the excellent old way through love,
And through the care of children, to the hour For bidding
Fate and Time and Change good-bye.

[MARY *stands for a moment in the door, and then takes
a sod of turf from the fire and goes out through the door.,*
SHAWN *follows her and meets her coming in.*]

SHAWN.

What is it draws you to the chill o' the wood?

There is a light among the stems of the trees
That makes one shiver.

> ### MARY.
>
> > A little queer old man
> Made me a sign to show he wanted fire
> To light his pipe.

> ### BRIDGET.
>
> > You've given milk and fire
> Upon the unluckiest night of the year and brought,
> For all you know, evil upon the house.
> Before you married you were idle and fine
> And went about with ribbons on your head;
> And now—no, Father, I will speak my mind—
> She is not a fitting wife for any man

> ### SHAWN.
>
> Be quiet, mother!

> ### MAURTEEN.
>
> > You are much too cross.

> ### MARY.
>
> What do I care if I have given this house,
> Where I must hear all day a bitter tongue,
> Into the power of faeries!

> ### BRIDGET.
>
> > You know well
> How calling the good people by that name,
> Or talking of them over much at all,
> May bring all kinds of evil on the house.

> ### MARY.
>
> Come, faeries, take me out of this dull house!
> Let me have all the freedom I have lost;
> Work when I will and idle when I will!
> Faeries, come take me out of this dull world,

For I would ride with you upon the wind,
Run on the top of the dishevelled tide, And
dance upon the mountains like a flame.

FATHER HART.

You cannot know the meaning of your words.

MARY.

Father, I am right weary of four tongues:
A tongue that is too crafty and too wise,
A tongue that is too godly and too grave,
A tongue that is more bitter than the tide,
And a kind tongue too full of drowsy love,
Of drowsy love and my captivity.
   [SHAWN BRUIN *leads her to a seat at the left of the
   door.*]

SHAWN.

Do not blame me; I often lie awake
Thinking that all things trouble your bright head.
How beautiful it is—your broad pale forehead
Under a cloudy blossoming of hair!
Sit down beside me here—these are too old,
And have forgotten they were ever young.

MARY.

O, you are the great door-post of this house,
And I the branch of blessed quicken wood,
And if I could I'd hang upon the post,
Till I had brought good luck into the house.
   [*She would put her arms about him, but looks shyly at
the priest and lets her arms fall.*]

FATHER HART.

My daughter, take his hand—by love alone
God binds us to Himself and to the hearth,
That shuts us from the waste beyond His peace,
From maddening freedom and bewildering light.

SHAWN.

Would that the world were mine to give it you,
And not its quiet hearths alone, but even
All that bewilderment of light and freedom,
If you would have it.

MARY.

              I would take the world And break
it into pieces in my hands
To see you smile watching it crumble away.

SHAWN.

Then I would mould a world of fire and dew, With
no one bitter, grave or over wise,
And nothing marred or old to do you wrong, And
crowd the enraptured quiet of the sky With candles
burning to your lonely face.

MARY.

Your looks are all the candles that I need.

SHAWN.

Once a fly dancing in a beam of the sun,
Or the light wind blowing out of the dawn,
Could fill your heart with dreams none other knew,
But now the indissoluble sacrament
Has mixed your heart that was most proud and cold
With my warm heart for ever; the sun and moon
Must fade and heaven be rolled up like a scroll;
But your white spirit still walks by my spirit.
      [A Voice singing in the wood.]

MAURTEEN.

There's some one singing.
             Why, it's but a child.
It sang, 'The lonely of heart is withered away.'
A strange song for a child, but she sings sweetly.
Listen, listen!   *[Goes to door.]*

MARY.

                 0, cling close to me,
Because I have said wicked things to-night.

THE VOICE.

The wind blows out of the gates of the day,
The wind blows over the lonely of heart,
And the lonely of heart is withered away.
While the faeries dance in a place apart,
Shaking their milk-white feet in a ring,
Tossing their milk-white arms in the air;
For they hear the wind laugh and murmur and sing
Of a land where even the old are fair,
And even the wise are merry of tongue;
But I heard a reed of Coolaney say,
'When the wind has laughed and murmured and sung
The lonely of heart is withered away!'

MAURTEEN.

Being happy, I would have all others happy,
So I will bring her in out of the cold.
[He brings in the faery child.]

THE CHILD.

I tire of winds and waters and pale lights.

MAURTEEN.

And that's no wonder, for when night has fallen
The wood's a cold and a bewildering place,
But you are welcome here.

THE CHILD.

                I am welcome here.
For when I tire of this warm little house
But there is one here that must away, away.

MAURTEEN.

O, listen to her dreamy and strange talk.
Are you not cold?

THE CHILD.

I will crouch down beside you,
For I have run a long, long way this night.

BRIDGET.

You have a comely shape.

MAURTEEN.

Your hair is wet.

BRIDGET.

I'll warm your chilly feet.

MAURTEEN.

You have come indeed
A long, long way—for I have never seen
Your pretty face—and must be tired and hungry,
Here is some bread and wine.

THE CHILD.

The wine is bitter.
Old mother, have you no sweet food for me?

BRIDGET.

I have some honey.
[She goes into the next room.]

MAURTEEN.

You have coaxing ways,
The mother was quite cross before you came.
[BRIDGET *returns with the honey and fills a por-*
ringer with milk.]

BRIDGET.

She is the child of gentle people; look
At her white hands and at her pretty dress.

I've brought you some new milk, but wait a while
And I will put it to the fire to warm,
For things well fitted for poor folk like us
Would never please a high-born child like you.

THE CHILD.

From dawn, when you must blow the fire ablaze,
You work your fingers to the bone, old mother.
The young may lie in bed and dream and hope,
But you must work your fingers to the bone
Because your heart is old.

BRIDGET.

The young are idle.

THE CHILD.

Your memories have made you wise, old father;
The young must sigh through many a dream and hope,
But you are wise because your heart is old.
  [BRIDGET *gives her more bread and honey.]*

MAURTEEN.

O, who would think to find so young a girl
Loving old age and wisdom?

THE CHILD.

No more, mother.

MAURTEEN.

What a small bite!   The milk is ready now.
[Hands it to her.]
 What a small sip!

THE CHILD.

Put on my shoes, old mother.
For I would like to dance now I have eaten,
The reeds are dancing by Coolaney lake,

And I would like to dance until the reeds
And the white waves have danced themselves asleep.
    [BRIDGET *puts on the shoes, and the* CHILD *is about
to dance, but suddenly sees the crucifix and shrieks
and covers her eyes.*]
    What is that ugly thing on the black cross?

FATHER HART.
You cannot know how naughty your words
are! That is our Blessed Lord.

THE CHILD.
Hide it away!

BRIDGET.
I have begun to be afraid again.

THE CHILD.
Hide it away!

MAURTEEN.
That would be wickedness!

BRIDGET.
That would be sacrilege!

THE CHILD.
The tortured thing!
Hide it away!

MAURTEEN.
Her parents are to blame.

FATHER HART.
That is the image of the Son of God.

THE CHILD *[caressing him]*.
Hide it away, hide it away!

MAURTEEN.
No, no.

FATHER HART.

Because you are so young and like a bird,
That must take fright at every stir of the leaves.
I will go take it down.

THE CHILD.
Hide it away!
And cover it out of sight and out of
mind!
    [FATHER HART *takes crucifix from wall and car-
ries it towards inner room.]*

FATHER HART.

Since you have come into this barony,
I will instruct you in our blessed faith;
And being so keen witted you'll soon learn.
    [To the others.)
We must be tender to all budding things,
Our Maker let no thought of Calvary
Trouble the morning stars in their first
song. *[Puts crucifix in inner room.]*

THE CHILD.

Here is level ground for dancing; I will dance.
    [Sings]
The wind blows out of the gates of the day,
The wind blows over the lonely of heart,
And the lonely of heart is withered away.
    [She dances.]

MARY *[to* SHAWN],
Just now when she came near I thought I heard
Other small steps beating upon the floor,
And a faint music blowing in the wind,
Invisible pipes giving her feet the tune.

SHAWN.

I heard no steps but hers.

MARY.
I hear them now,
The unholy powers are dancing in the house.

MAURTEEN.
Come over here, and if you promise me
Not to talk wickedly of holy things
I will give you something.

THE CHILD.
Bring it me, old father.

MAURTEEN.
Here are some ribbons that I bought in the town
For my son's wife—but she will let me give them
To tie up that wild hair the winds have tumbled.

THE CHILD.
Come, tell me, do you love me?

MAURTEEN.
Yes, I love you.

THE CHILD.
Ah, but you love this fire-side. Do you love me?

FATHER HART.
When the Almighty puts so great a share
Of his own ageless youth into a creature,
To look is but to love.

THE CHILD.
But you love Him?

BRIDGET.
She is blaspheming.

THE CHILD.
And do you love me too?

MARY.
I do not know.

THE CHILD.
You love that young man there, Yet I
could make you ride upon the winds,
Run on the top of the dishevelled tide,
And dance upon the mountains like a flame.

MARY.
Queen of Angels and kind saints defend us! Some
dreadful thing will happen. A while ago She took
away the blessed quicken wood.

FATHER HART.
You fear because of her unmeasured prattle;
She knows no better.   Child, how old are you?

THE CHILD.
When winter sleep is abroad my hair grows thin,
My feet unsteady. When the leaves awaken
My mother carries me in her golden arms;
I'll soon put on my womanhood and marry
The spirits of wood and water, but who can tell
When I was born for the first time?
I think I am much older than the eagle cock
That blinks and blinks on Ballygawley Hill,
And he is the oldest thing under the moon.

FATHER HART.
O, she is of the faery people.

THE CHILD.
One called,
I sent my messengers for milk and fire,
She called again and after that I came.

[All except SHAWN *and* MARY BRUIN *gather behind the priest for protection.]*

SHAWN *[rising]*.

Though you have made all these obedient, You
have not charmed my sight and won from me
A wish or gift to make you powerful;
I'll turn you from the house.

FATHER HART.

No, I will face her.

THE CHILD.

Because you took away the crucifix
I am so mighty that there's none can pass,
Unless I will it, where my feet have danced
Or where I've whirled my finger-tops.

[SHAWN *tries to approach her and cannot.]*

MAURTEEN.

Look, look!
There something stops him—look how he moves his hands
As though he rubbed them on a wall of glass!

FATHER HART.

I will confront this mighty spirit alone;
Be not afraid, the Father is with us,
The Holy Martyrs and the Innocents,
The adoring Magi in their coats of mail,
And He who died and rose on the third day,
And all the nine angelic hierarchies.
[The CHILD *kneels upon the settle beside* MARY *and
puts her arms about her.]*
Cry, daughter, to the Angels and the Saints.

THE CHILD.

You shall go with me, newly-married
bride, And gaze upon a merrier multitude.

White-armed Nuala, Aengus of the Birds,
Feacra of the hurtling foam, and him
Who is the ruler of the Western Host,
 Finvarra, and their Land of Heart's Desire,
Where beauty has no ebb, decay no flood,
But joy is wisdom, Time an endless song.
I kiss you and the world begins to fade.

SHAWN.

Awake out of that trance—and cover up
Your eyes and ears.

FATHER HART.

            She must both look and listen,
For only the soul's choice can save her now.
Come over to me, daughter; stand beside me;
Think of this house and of your duties in it.

THE CHILD.

Stay and come with me, newly-married bride,
For if you hear him you grow like the rest;
Bear children, cook, and bend above the churn,
And wrangle over butter, fowl, and eggs,
Until at last, grown old and bitter of tongue,
You're crouching there and shivering at the grave.

FATHER HART.

Daughter, I point you out the way to Heaven.

THE CHILD.

But I can lead you, newly-married bride,
Where nobody gets old and crafty and wise,
Where nobody gets old and godly and grave,
Where nobody gets old and bitter of tongue,
And where kind tongues bring no captivity;
For we are but obedient to the thoughts
That drift into the mind at a wink of the eye.

FATHER HART.

By the dear Name of the One crucified,
I bid you, Mary Bruin, come to me.

THE CHILD.

I keep you in the name of your own heart.

FATHER HART.

It is because I put away the crucifix
That I am nothing, and my power is nothing.
I'll bring it here again.

MAURTEEN *[clinging to him].*

No.

BRIDGET.

Do not leave us.

FATHER HART.

O, let me go before it is too late;
It is my sin alone that brought it all.
[Singing outside.]

THE CHILD.

I hear them sing, 'Come, newly-married bride,
Come, to the woods and waters and pale lights.'

MARY.

I will go with you.

FATHER HART.

She is lost, alas!

THE CHILD *[standing by the door].*

But clinging mortal hope must fall from you,
For we who ride the winds, run on the waves,
And dance upon the mountains are more light
Than dewdrops on the banner of the dawn.

MARY.

O, take me with you.

SHAWN.
Beloved, I will keep you.
I've more than words, I have these arms to hold you,
Nor all the faery host, do what they please,
Shall ever make me loosen you from these arms.

MARY.

Dear face! Dear voice!

THE CHILD.
Come, newly-married bride.

MARY.
I always loved her world—and yet—and yet

THE CHILD.
White bird, white bird, come with me, little bird.

MARY.
She calls me!

THE CHILD.
Come with me, little bird.
[Distant dancing figures appear in the wood.]

MARY.
I can hear songs and dancing.

SHAWN.
Stay with me.

MARY.
I think that I would stay—and yet—and yet-

THE CHILD.
Come, little bird with crest of gold.

MARY *[very softly]*.
And yet ---

THE CHILD.
Come, little bird with silver feet!

[MARY BRUIN *dies and the* CHILD *goes.]*

SHAWN.

She is dead!

BRIDGET.
Come from that image; body and soul are gone.
You have thrown your arms about a drift of leaves,
Or bole of an ash-tree changed into her image.

FATHER HART.
Thus do the spirits of evil snatch their prey,
Almost out of the very hand of God;
 And day by day their power is more and more,
And men and women leave old paths, for pride
Comes knocking with thin knuckles on the heart.
    [Outside there are dancing figures, and it may be
a white bird, and many voices singing:]
The wind blows out of the gates of the day,
The wind blows over the lonely of heart,
And the lonely of heart is withered away;
While the faeries dance in a place apart,
Shaking their milk-white feet in a ring,
Tossing their milk-white arms in the air;
For they hear the wind laugh and murmur and sing
Of a land where even the old are fair,
And even the wise are merry of tongue;
But I heard a reed of Coolaney say
'When the wind has laughed and murmured and
sung, The lonely of heart is withered away.'

NOTE

This little play was produced at the Avenue Theatre in the spring of 1894, with the following cast:—Maurteen Bruin, Mr. James Welch; Shawn Bruin, Mr. A. E. W. Mason; Father Hart, Mr. G. R. Foss; Bridget Bruin, Miss Charlotte Morland; Mary Bruin, Miss Winifred Fraser; A Faery Child, Miss Dorothy Paget. It ran for a little over six weeks. It was revived in America in 1901, when it was taken on tour by Mrs. Lemoyne. It has been played two or three times professionally since then in America, and a great many times in England and America by amateurs. Till lately it was not part of the repertory of the Abbey Theatre, for I had grown to dislike it without knowing what I disliked in it. This winter, however, I have made many revisions, and now it plays well enough to give me pleasure. It is printed in this book in the new form, which was acted for the first time on February 22, 1912, at the Abbey Theatre, Dublin. At the Abbey Theatre, where the platform of the stage comes out in front of the curtain, the curtain falls before the priest's last words. He remains outside the curtain and the words are spoken to the audience like an epilogue.—W. B. Y., 1912.

THE TWISTING OF THE ROPE

A Comedy in One Act

BY **DOUGLAS HYDE**

DRAMATIS PERSONS

HANRAHAN, *a wandering poet.*

MAURYA, *the woman of the house.*

SHEELA, *a neighbor.*

SHEAMUS O' Heran, *engaged to Oona.*

OONA, *Maurya's daughter.*

Neighbors and a piper who have come to MAURYA'S *house for a dance.*

SCENE: *A farmer's house in Munster a hundred years ago. Men and women moving about and standing round the walls as if they had just finished a dance,* HANRAHAN, *in the foreground, talking to* OONA.

The piper is beginning a preparatory drone for another dance, but SHEAMUS *brings him a drink and he stops. A man has come and holds out his hand to* OONA, *as if to lead her out, but she pushes him away.*

OONA. Don't be bothering me now; don't you see I'm listening to what he is saying? *[To* HANRAHAN.] Go on with what you were saying just now.

HANRAHAN. What did that fellow want of you?

OONA. He wanted the next dance with me, but I wouldn't give it to him.

HANRAHAN. And why would you give it to him? Do you think I'd let you dance with anyone but myself, and I here? I had no comfort or satisfaction this long time until I came here tonight, and till I saw yourself.

OONA. What comfort am I to you?

HANRAHAN. When a stick is half burned in the fire, does it not get comfort when water is poured on it?

38

OONA.   But, sure, you are not half burned.

HANRAHAN. I am; and three-quarters of my heart is burned, and scorched and consumed, struggling with the world, and the world struggling with me.

OONA.   You don't look that bad.

HANRAHAN. 0, Oona ni Regaun, you have not knowledge of the life of a poor bard, without house or havings, but he going and ever going a drifting through the wide world, without a person with him but himself. There is not a morning in the week when I rise up that I do not say to myself that it would be better to be in the grave than to be wandering. There is nothing standing to me but the gift I got from God, my share of songs; when I begin upon them, my grief and my trouble go from me; I forget my persecution and my ill luck; and now since I saw you, Oona, I see there is something that is better even than the songs.

OONA. Poetry is a wonderful gift from God; and as long as you have that, you are richer than the people of stock and store, the people of cows and cattle.

HANRAHAN. Ah, Oona, it is a great blessing, but it is a great curse as well for a man, he to be a poet. Look at me: have I a friend in this world? Is there a man alive that has a wish for me? is there the love of anyone at all on me? I am going like a poor lonely barnacle goose throughout the world; like Oisin after the Fenians; every person hates me: you do not hate me, Oona?

OONA. Do not say a thing like that; it is impossible that anyone would hate you.

HANRAHAN. Come and we will sit in the corner of the room together; and I will tell you the little song I made for you; it is for you I made it. *[They go to a corner and sit down together,* SHEELA *comes in at the door.]*

SHEELA.   I came to you as quick as I could.

MAURYA.   And a hundred welcomes to you.

SHEELA.   What have you going on now?

MAURYA. Beginning we are; we had one jig, and now the piper is drinking a glass. They'll begin dancing again in a minute when the piper is ready.

SHEELA. There are a good many people gathering in to you tonight. We will have a fine dance.

MAURYA. Maybe so, Sheela; but there's a man of them there, and I'd sooner him out than in.

SHEELA. It's about the long red man you are talking, isn't it — the man that is in close talk with Oona in the corner? Where is he from, and who is he himself?

MAURYA. That's the greatest vagabond ever came into Ireland; Tumaus Hanrahan they call him; but it's Hanrahan the rogue he ought to have been christened by right. Aurah, wasn't there the misfortune on me, him to come in to us at all tonight?

SHEELA. What sort of a person is he? Isn't he a man that makes songs, out of Connacht? I heard talk of him before; and they say there is not another dancer in Ireland so good as him. I would like to see him dance.

MAURYA. Bad luck to the vagabond! It is well I know what sort he is; because there was a kind of friendship between himself and the first husband I had; and it is often I heard from poor Diarmuid— the Lord have mercy on him!— what sort of a person he was. He was a schoolmaster down in Connacht; but he used to have every trick worse than another; ever making songs he used to be, and drinking whiskey and setting quarrels afoot among the neighbors with his share of talk. They say there isn't a woman in the five provinces that he wouldn't deceive. He is worse than Donal na Greina long ago. But the end of the story is that the priest routed him out of the parish altogether; he got another place then, and followed on at the same tricks until he was routed out again, and another again with it. Now he has neither place nor house nor anything, but he to be going the country, making songs and getting a night's lodging from the people; nobody will refuse him, because they are afraid of him. He's a great poet, and maybe he'd make a rann on you that would stick to you for ever, if you were to anger him.

SHEELA. God preserve us; but what brought him in tonight?

MAURYA. He was traveling the country and he heard there was to be a dance here, and he came in because he knew us; he was rather great with my first husband. It is wonderful how he is making out his way of life at all, and he with nothing but his share of songs. They say there is no place that he'll go to, that the women don't love him, and that the men don't hate him.

SHEELA *[catching* MAURYA *by the shoulder]*. Turn your head, Maurya; look at him now, himself and your daughter, and their heads together; he's whispering in her ear; he's after making a poem for her and he's whispering it in her ear. Oh, the villain, he'll be putting his spells on her now.

MAURYA. Ohone, go deo! isn't it a misfortune that he came? He's talking every moment with Oona since he came in three hours ago. I did my best to separate them from one another, but it failed me. Poor Oona is given up to every sort of old songs and old made-up stories; and she thinks it sweet to be listening to him. The marriage is settled between herself and Sheamus O'Heran there, a quarter from today. Look at poor Sheamus at the door, and he watching them. There is grief and hanging of the head on him; it's easy to see that he'd like to choke the vagabond this minute. I am greatly afraid that the head will be turned on Oona with his share of blathering. As sure as I am alive there will come evil out of this night.

SHEELA. And couldn't you put him out?

MAURYA. I could. There's no person here to help him unless there would be a woman or two; but he is a great poet, and he has a curse that would split the trees, and that would burst the stones. They say the seed will rot in the ground and the milk go from the cows when a poet like him makes a curse, if a person routed him out of the house; but if he was once out, I'll go bail I wouldn't let him in again.

SHEELA. If himself were to go out willingly, there would be no virtue in his curse then.

MAURYA. There would not, but he will not go out willingly, and I cannot rout him out myself for fear of his curse.

SHEELA. Look at poor Sheamus. He is going over to her. [SHEAMUS *gets up and goes over to her.*]

SHEAMUS. Will you dance this reel with me, Oona, as soon as the piper is ready?

HANRAHAN *[rising up]*. I am Tumaus Hanrahan, and I am speaking now to Oona ni Regaun; and as she is willing to be talking to me, I will allow no living person to come between us.

SHEAMUS *[without heeding* HANRAHAN]. Will you not dance with me, Oona?

HANRAHAN *[savagely]*. Didn't I tell you now that it was to me Oona ni Regaun was talking? Leave that on the spot, you clown, and do not raise a disturbance here.

SHEAMUS.   Oona -

HANRAHAN *[shouting]*. Leave that! [SHEAMUS *goes away, and comes over to the two old women.*]

SHEAMUS. Maurya Regaun, I am asking leave of you to throw that ill-mannerly, drunken vagabond out of the house. Myself and my two brothers will put him out if you will allow us; and when he's outside I'll settle with him.

MAURYA. Sheamus, do not; I am afraid of him. That man has a curse they say that would split the trees.

SHEAMUS. I don't care if he had a curse that would overthrow the heavens; it is on me it will fall, and I defy him! If he were to kill me on the moment, I will not allow him to put his spells on Oona. Give me leave, Maurya.

SHEELA. Do not, Sheamus. I have a better advice than that.

SHEAMUS. What advice is that?

SHEELA. I have a way in my head to put him out. If you follow my advice, he will go out himself as quiet as a lamb; and when you get him out, slap the door on him, and never let him in again.

MAURYA. Luck from God to you, Sheela, and tell us what's in your head.

SHEELA. We will do it as nice and easy as you ever saw. We will put him to twist a hay-rope till he is outside, and then we will shut the door on him.

SHEAMUS. It's easy to say, but not easy to do. He will say to you, 'Make a hay-rope yourself.'

SHEELA. We will say then that no one ever saw a hay-rope made, that there is no one at all in the house to make the beginning of it.

SHEAMUS. But will *he* believe that we never saw a hay-rope?

SHEELA. He believe it, is it? He'd believe anything; he'd believe that himself is king over Ireland when he has a glass taken, as he has now.

SHEAMUS. But what excuse can we make for saying we want a hay-rope?

MAURYA. Can't you think of something yourself, Sheamus?

SHEAMUS. Sure, I can say the wind is rising, and I must bind the thatch, or it will be off the house.

SHEELA. But he'll know the wind is not rising if he does but listen at the door. You must think of some other excuse, Sheamus.

SHEAMUS. Wait, I have a good idea now; say there is a coach upset at the bottom of the hill, and that they are asking for a hay-rope to mend it with. He can't see as far as that from the door, and he won't know it's not true it is.

MAURYA. That's the story, Sheela. Now, Sheamus, go among the people and tell them the secret. Tell them what they have to say, what no one at all in this country ever saw a hay-rope, and put a good skin on the lie yourself, [SHEA-MUS *goes from person to person whispering to them, and some begin laughing. The piper has begun playing. Three or jour couples rise up.]*

HANRAIIAN *[after looking at them for a couple of minutes}*. Whisht! Let ye sit down! Do you call that dragging, dancing? You are tramping the floor like so many cattle. You are as heavy as bullocks, as awkward as asses. May my throat be choked if I would not sooner be looking at as many lame ducks hopping on one leg through the house. Leave the floor to Oona ni Regaun and to me.

ONE OF THE MEN GOING TO DANCE.   And for

what WOUld

we leave the floor to you?

HANRAHAN. The swan of the brink of the waves, the royal phoenix, the pearl of the white breast, the Venus amongst the women, Oona ni Regaun, is standing up with me, and any place she rises up, the sun and the moon bow to her, and so shall ye yet. She is too handsome, too sky-like for any other woman to be near her. But wait a while! Before I'll show you how the Connacht boy can dance, I will give you the poem I made on the star of the province of Munster, on Oona ni Regaun. Get up, O sun among women, and we will sing the song together, verse about, and then we'll show them what right dancing is!   [OONA *rises.]*

HANRAHAN She is white Oona of the yellow hair, The Coolin that was destroying my heart inside me; She is my secret love and my lasting affection; I care not for ever for any woman but her.

OONA

O bard of the black eye, it is you Who have found victory in the world and fame;

I call on yourself and I praise your mouth;
You have set my heart in my breast astray.

HANRAHAN

0 fair Oona of the golden hair,
My desire, my affection, my love and my store,
Herself will go with her bard afar;
She has hurt his heart in his breast greatly.

OONA

1 would not think the night long nor the day,
Listening to your fine discourse;
More melodious is your mouth than the singing of
From my heart in my breast you have found love.

HANRAHAN

I walked myself the entire world,
England, Ireland, France, and Spain;
I never saw at home or afar
Any girl under the sun like fair Oona.

OONA

I have heard the melodious harp
On the streets of Cork playing to us;
More melodious by far I thought your voice,
More melodious by far your mouth than that.

HANRAHAN

I was myself one time a poor barnacle goose;
The night was not plain to me more than the day
Till I got sight of her; she is the love of my heart
That banished from me my grief and my misery.

OONA

I was myself on the morning of yesterday
Walking beside the wood at the break of day;
There was a bird there was singing sweetly,
How I love love, and is it not beautiful?

[A shout and a noise, and SHEAMUS O'HERAN
rushes in.]
SHEAMUS. Ububul Ohone-y-o, go deo! The big
coach is overthrown at the foot of the hill! The bag
in which the letters of the country are is bursted;
and there is neither tie, nor cord, nor rope, nor anything to bind it up. They are calling out now for a
hay sugaun—whatever kind of thing that is; the letters and the coach will be lost for want of a hay
sugaun to bind them.

HANRAHAN. Do not be bothering us; we have our
poem done, and we are going to dance. The coach
does not come this way at all.

SHEAMUS. The coach does come this way now;
but sure you're a stranger, and you don't know.
Doesn't the coach come over the hill now, neighbors?

ALL.   It does, it does, surely.

HANRAHAN. I don't care whether it does come or
whether it doesn't. I would sooner twenty coaches
to be overthrown on the road than the pearl of the
white breast to be stopped from dancing to us. Tell
the coachman to twist a rope for himself.

SHEAMUS. Oh! murder 1 he can't. There's that
much vigor, and fire, and activity, and courage in
the horses, that my poor coachman must take them
by the heads; it's on the pinch of his life he's able to
control them; he's afraid of his soul they'll go from
him of a rout. They are neighing like anything; you
never saw the like of them for wild horses.

HANRAHAN. Are there no other people in the
coach that will make a rope, if the coachman has to
be at the horses' heads? Leave that, and let us
dance.

SHEAMUS. There are three others in it; but as to one of them, he is one-handed, and another man of them, he's shaking and trembling with the fright he got; it's not in him now to stand up on his two feet with the fear that's on him; and as for the third man, there isn't a person in this country would speak to him about a rope at all, for his own father was hanged with a rope last year for stealing sheep.

HANRAHAN. Then let one of yourselves twist a rope so, and leave the floor to us. *[To* OONA.*]* Now, O star of women, show me how Juno goes among the gods, or Helen for whom Troy was destroyed. By my word, since Deirdre died, for whom Naoise, son of Usnech, was put to death, her heir is not in Ireland today but yourself. Let us begin.

SHEAMUS. Do not begin until we have a rope; we are not able to twist a rope; there's nobody here can twist a rope.

HANRAHAN. There's nobody here is able to twist a rope?

ALL. Nobody at all.

SHEELA. And that's true; nobody in this place ever made a hay sugaun. I don't believe there's a person in this house who ever saw one itself but me. It's well I remember when I was a little girsha that I saw one of them on a goat that my grandfather brought with him out of Connacht. All the people used to be saying: "Aurah, what sort of a thing is that at all?" And he said that it was a sugaun that was in it; and that people used to make the like of that down in Connacht. He said that one man would go holding the hay, and another man twisting it. I'll hold the hay now; and you'll go twisting it.

SHEAMUS. I'll bring in a lock of hay. *[He goes out.]*

HANRAHAN

I will make a dispraising of the province of Munster:
They do not leave the floor to us;
It isn't in them to twist even a sugaun;
The province of Munster without nicety, without prosperity.

Disgust for ever on the province of Munster,
That they do not leave us the floor;
The province of Munster of the foul clumsy people.
They cannot even twist a sugaun!

SHEAMUS *[coming back].*   Here's the hay now.

HANRAHAN. Give it here to me; I'll show ye what the well-learned, hardy, honest, clever, sensible Connachtman will do, that has activity and full deftness in his hands, and sense in his head, and courage in his heart; but that the misfortune and the great trouble of the world directed him among the *lebidins* of the province of Munster, without honor, without nobility, without knowledge of the swan beyond the duck, or of the gold beyond the brass, or of the lily beyond the thistle, or of the star of young women, and the pearl of the white breast, beyond their own share of sluts and slatterns. Give me a kippeen. *[A man hands him a stick; he puts a wisp of hay round it, and begins twisting it; and* SHEELA *giving him out the hay.]*

HANRAHAN

There is a pearl of a woman giving light to us;
She is my love; she is my desire;
She is fair Oona, the gentle queen-woman.
And the Munstermen do not understand half her
courtesy.

These Munstermen are blinded by God;
They do not recognize the swan beyond the gray
duck;
But she will come with me, my fine Helen,
Where her person and her beauty shall be praised
forever.

Arrah, wisha, wisha, wisha! isn't this the fine village? isn't this the exceeding village? The village where there be that many rogues hanged that the people have no want of ropes with all the ropes that they steal from the hangman!

The sensible Connachtman makes
  A rope for himself;
But the Munsterman steals it
  From the hangman
That I may see a fine rope,
  A rope of hemp yet,
A stretching on the throats
  Of every person here!

On account of one woman only the Greeks de-
parted, and they never stopped, and they never
greatly stayed, till they destroyed Troy; and on account of one woman only this village shall be
damned; *go deo, ma neoir,* and to the womb of
judgment, by God of the graces, eternally and ever-
lastingly, because they did not understand that Oona
ni Regaun is the second Helen, who was born in
their midst, and that she overcame in beauty Deirdre and Venus, and all that came before or that will
come after her!
 But she will come with me, my pearl of a woman,
  To the province of Connacht of the fine people;
 She will receive feasts, wine, and meat,
  High dances, sport, and music!
Oh, wisha, wisha! that the sun may never rise upon this village;   and that the stars may never shine
on it; and
that ----.   *[He is by this time outside the door. All the
men make a rush at the door and shut it.* OONA *runs
towards the door, but the women seize her.*
SHEAMUS *goes over to her.]*
 OONA. Oh! oh! oh! do not put him out; let him
back; that is Tumaus Hanrahan—he is a poet—he is
a bard—he is a wonderful man. Oh, let him back!
do not do that to him!
 SHEAMUS. Oh, Oona *ban, acushla dilis,* let him
be; he is gone now, and his share of spells with
him!

He will be gone out of your head tomorrow; and you will be gone out of his head. Don't you know that I like you better than a hundred thousand Deirdres, and that you are my one pearl of a woman in the world?

HANRAHAN *[outside, beating on the door]*. Open, open, open; let me in! Oh, my seven hundred thousand curses on you—the curse of the weak and of the strong—the curse of the poets and of the bards upon you! The curse of the priests on you and the friars! The curse of the bishops upon you, and the Pope! The curse of the widows on you, and the children! Open! *[He beats on the door again and again.]*

SHEAMUS. I am thankful to ye, neighbors; and Oona will be thankful to ye tomorrow. Beat away, you vagabond! Do your dancing out there with yourself now! Isn't it a fine thing for a man to be listening to the storm outside, and himself quiet and easy beside the fire? Beat away, beat away! Where's Connacht now?

RIDERS TO THE SEA

A Tragic Drama in One Act

By **J. M. SYNGE**

DRAMATIS PERSONS

MAURYA   BARTLEY, *Her Sotl*
CATHLEEN   NORA
Her two Daughters
MEN and WOMEN

SCENE—*Island off the West of Ireland. Cottage kitchen, with nets, oil-skins, spinning wheel, some new boards standing by the wall, etc.* CATHLEEN, *a girl oj about twenty, finishes kneading cake, and puts it down in the pot-oven by the fire; then wipes her hands, and begins to spin at the wheel,* NORA, *a young girl, puts her head in at the door.*

NORA *[in a low voice].* Where is she?

CATHLEEN. She's lying down, God help her, and maybe sleeping, if she's able.

[NORA *comes in softly, and takes a bundle from tinder her shawl.]*

CATHLEEN *[spinning the wheel rapidly].* What is it you have?

NORA. The young priest is after bringing them. It's a shirt and a plain stocking were got off a drowned man in Donegal.

[CATHLEEN *stops her wheel with a sudden movement, and leans out to listen.]*

NORA. We're to find out if it's Michael's they are, some time herself will be down looking by the sea.

CATHLEEN. How would they be Michael's, Nora? How would he go the length of that way to the far north?

NORA. The young priest says he's known the like of it. Tf it's Michael's they are,' says he, 'you can tell herself he's got a clean burial by the grace of God, and if they're not his let no one say a word

52

about them for she'll be getting her death,' says he, 'with crying and lamenting.'
[The door which NORA *half closed behind her is blown open by a gust of wind.]*

CATHLEEN *[looking out anxiously].* Did you ask him would he stop Bartley going this day to Connemara?

NORA. 'I won't stop him,' says he, 'but let you not be afraid. Herself does be saying prayers half through the night, and the Almighty God won't leave her destitute,' says he, 'with no son living.'

CATHLEEN. Is the sea bad by the white rocks, Nora?

NORA. Middling bad, God help us. There's a great roaring in the west, and it's worse it'll be getting when the tide's turned to the wind. *[She goes over to the table with the bundle.]*   Shall I open it now?

CATHLEEN. Maybe she'd wake up on us, and come in before we'd done. *[Coming to the table]*— It's a long time we'll be, and the two of us crying.

NORA *[goes to the inner door and listens].* She's moving about on the bed.   She'll be coming in a minute.

CATHLEEN. Give me the ladder, and I'll put them up in the turf-loft, the way she won't know of them at all, and maybe when the tide turns she'll be going down to see would he be floating from the east.

[They put the ladder against the gable of the chimney, and CATHLEEN *goes up under the thatch with the bundle in her hand,* MAURYA, *the old woman, comes from the inner roo7n.]*

MAURYA *[looking up at* CATHLEEN *and speaking querulously].* Isn't it turf enough you have for this day and evening?

CATHLEEN. There's a cake baking at the fire for a short space *[throwing down turf],* and Bartley will want it when the tide turns if he goes to Connemara.

*[*NORA *picks up the turf and puts it round the pot-oven.]*

MAURYA *[sitting down on a stool at the fire]*. He won't go this day with the wind rising from the south and west. He won't go this day, for the young priest will stop him surely.

NORA. He'll not stop him, mother, and I heard Eamon Simon and Stephen Pheety and Colum Shawn saying he would go.

MAURYA. Where is he itself?

NORA. He went down to see would there be another boat sailing in the week, and I'm thinking it won't be long till he's here now, for the tide's turning at the green head, and the hooker's tacking from the east.

CATHLEEN. I hear someone passing the big stones.

NORA *[looking out]*. He's coming now, and he is in a hurry.

BARTLEY *[comes in and looks around the room. Speaking sadly and quietly]*. Where is the bit of new rope, Cathleen, was bought in Connemara?

CATHLEEN *[coming down]*. Give it to him, Nora; it's on a nail by the white boards. I hung it up this morning, for the pig with the black feet was eating it.

NORA *[giving him a rope]*. Is that it, Bartley?

MAURYA. You'd do right to leave that rope, Bartley, hanging by the boards, [BARTLEY *takes the rope.*] It will be wanting in this place, I'm telling you, if Michael is washed up tomorrow morning, or the next morning, or any morning in the week, for it's a deep grave we'll make him by the grace of God.

BARTLEY *[beginning to work with the rope]*. I've no halter the way I can ride down on the mare, and I must go now quickly. This is the one boat going for two weeks or beyond it, and the fare will be a good fare I heard them saying below.

MAURYA. It's a hard thing they'll be saying below if the body is washed up and there's no man in it to make the coffin, and I after giving a big price for the finest white boards you'ld find in Connemara. *[She looks round at the boards.]*

BARTLEY. How would it be washed up, and we after looking each day for nine days, and a strong wind blowing a while back from the west and south?

MAURYA. If it isn't found itself, that wind is raising the sea, and there was a star up against the moon, and it rising in the night. If it was a hundred horses, or a thousand horses you had itself, what is the price of a thousand horses against a son where there is one son only?

BARTLEY *[working at the halter, to* CATHLEEN*]*. Let you go down each day, and see the sheep aren't jumping in on the rye, and if the jobber comes you can sell the pig with the black feet if there is a good price going.

MAURYA. How would the like of her get a good price for a pig?

BARTLEY *[to* CATHLEEN*]*. If the west wind holds with the last bit of the moon, let you and Nora get up weed enough for another cock for the kelp—It's hard sot we'll be from this day with no one in it but one man to work.

MAURYA. It's hard set we'll be surely the day you're drown'd with the rest. What way will I live and the girls with me, and I an old woman looking for the grave?

[BARTLEY lays down the halter; takes off his old coat, and puts on a newer one of the same flannel.]

BARTLEY *[to* NORA*]*. Is she coming to the pier?

NORA *[looking out]*. She's passing the green head and letting fall her sails.

BARTLEY *[getting his purse and tobacco]*. I'll have half an hour to go down, and you'll see me coming again in two days, or in three days, or maybe in four days if the wind is bad

MAURYA *[turning round to the fire and putting her shawl over her head]*. Isn't it a hard and cruel man won't hear a word from an old woman, and she's holding him from the sea?

CATHLEEN. It's the life of a young man to be going on the sea, and who would listen to an old woman with one thing and she saying it over?

BARTLEY *[taking the halter]*. I must go now quickly. I'll ride down on the red mare, and the gray pony'll run behind me. . . . The blessing of God on you. . . . *[He goes out.]*

MAURYA *[crying out as he is in the door]*. He's gone now, God spare us, and we'll not see him again. He's gone now and when the black night is falling I'll have no son left me in the world.

CATHLEEN. Why wouldn't you give him your blessing and he looking round in the door? Isn't sorrow enough is on everyone in this house without your sending him out with an unlucky word behind him and a hard word in his ear?

[MAURYA takes up the tongs and begins raking the fire aimlessly without looking round.]

NORA *[turning towards her]*. You're taking away the turf from the cake.

CATHLEEN *[crying out]*. The Son of God forgive us, we're after forgetting his bit of bread. *[She comes over to the fire.]*

NORA. And it's destroyed he'll be going till dark night, and he after eating nothing since the sun went up.

CATHLEEN *[turning the cake out of the oven]*. It's destroyed he'll be, surely. . . . There's no sense left on any person in house where an old woman will be talking forever.

[MAURYA sways herself on her stool.]

CATHLEEN *[cuts off some of the bread and rolls it in a cloth; to* MAURYA *]*. Let you go down now to the spring well and give him this and he passing. You'll see him then and the dark word will be broken and you can say 'God speed you,' the way he'll be easy in his mind.

MAURYA *[taking the bread]*.... Will I be in it as soon as himself?

CATHLEEN. ... If you go now quickly.

MAURYA *[standing up unsteadily]*.... It's hard set I am to walk.

CATHLEEN *[looking at her anxiously]*.... Give her the stick, Nora, or maybe she'll slip on the big stones.

NORA. What stick?

CATHLEEN. The stick Michael brought from Connemara.

MAURYA *[taking a stick NORA gives her]*.... In the big world the old people do be leaving things after them for their sons and children, but in this place it is the young men do be leaving things behind for them that do be old. *[She goes out slowly.]*

[NORA goes over to the ladder.]

CATHLEEN. Wait, Nora, maybe she'd turn back quickly. She's that sorry, God help her, you wouldn't know the thing she'd do.

NORA. Is she gone round by the bush?

CATHLEEN *[looking out]*. She's gone now. Throw it down quickly, for the Lord knows when she'll be out of it again.

NORA *[getting the bundle from the loft]*. The young priest said he'd be passing tomorrow, and we might go down and speak to him below if it's Michael's they are surely . . .

CATHLEEN *[taking the bundle]*. Did he say what way they were found?

NORA *[coming down]*. 'There were two men,' says he, 'and they rowing round with poteen before the cocks crowed, and the oar of one of them caught the body and they passing the black cliffs of the north.'

CATHLEEN *[trying to open the bundle]*. Give me a knife, Nora, the string's perished with the salt water, and there's a black knot on it you wouldn't loosen in a week.

NORA *[giving her a knife]*. I've heard tell it was a
long way to Donegal. . . .

CATHLEEN *[cutting the string]*. It is surely. There
was a man in here a while ago—the man sold us
that knife—and he said if you set off walking from
the rocks beyond, it would be in seven days you'd
be in Donegal.

NORA. And what time would a man take and he
floating?

*[CATHLEEN opens the bundle and takes out a bit
of a shirt and a stocking. They look at them eager-
ly.]*

CATHLEEN *[in a low voice]*. The Lord spare us,
Nora; isn't it a queer hard thing to say if it's his they
are surely?

NORA. I'll get his shirt off the hook the way we
can put the one flannel on the other. *[She looks
through some clothes hanging in the corner.]* It's
not with them, Cathleen, and where will it be?

CATHLEEN. I'm thinking Bartley put it on him in
the morning, for his own shirt was heavy with the
salt in it *[pointing to the corner]*. There's a bit of a
sleeve was of the same stuff. Give me that and it
will do.

*[NORA brings it to her and they compare the flan-
nel.]*

CATHLEEN. . . . It's the same stuff, Nora; but if it
is itself, aren't there great rolls of it in the shops of
Galway, and isn't it many another man may have a
shirt of it as well as Michael himself?

NORA *[who has taken up the stocking and count-
ed the stitches, crying out.]* It's Michael's, Cathleen,
it's Michael's; God spare his soul, and what will
herself say when she hears this story and Bartley on
the sea?

CATHLEEN *[taking the stocking.]* It's a plain
stocking.

NORA. It's the second one of the third pair I knit-
ted, and I put up threescore stitches, and I dropped
four of them.

CATHLEEN *[counts the stitches]*.... It's that number
is in it. *[Crying out]* Ah, Nora, isn't it a bitter thing
to think of him floating that way to the far north,
and no one to keen him but the black hags that do
be flying on the sea?

NORA *[swinging herself half round, and throwing out her arm on the clothes]*.... And isn't it a pitiful thing when there is nothing left of a man who was a great rower and fisher, but a bit of an old shirt and a plain stocking?

CATHLEEN *[after an instant]*.... Tell me is herself coming, Nora? I hear a little sound on the path.

NORA *[looking out]*. . . . She is, Cathleen. She's coming up to the door.

CATHLEEN. Put these things away before she'll come in. Maybe it's easier she'll be after giving her blessing to Bart-ley, and we won't let on we've heard anything the time he's on the sea.

NORA *[helping* CATHLEEN *to close the bundle]*. We'll put them here in the corner. *[They put them into a hole in the chimney corner,* CATHLEEN *goes back to the spinning wheel.]*

NORA.   Will she see it was crying I was?

CATHLEEN. Keep your back to the door the way the light'll not be on you.

*[*NORA *sits down at the chimney corner, with her back to the door,* MAURYA *comes in very slowly, without looking at the girls, and goes over to her stool at the other side of the fire. The cloth with the bread is still in her hand. The girls look at each other, and* NORA *points to the bundle of bread.]*

CATHLEEN *[after spinning for a moment]*. . . . You didn't give him his bit of bread?

*[*MAURYA *begins to keen softly, withotit turning round.]*

CATHLEEN.   Did you see him riding down?

*[*MAURYA *goes on keening.]*

CATHLEEN *[a little impatiently]*. God forgive you; isn't it a better thing to raise your voice and tell what you've seen, than to be making lamentation for a thing that's done? Did you see Bartley, I'm saying to you?

MAURYA *[with a weak voice]*. My heart's broken from this day.

CATHLEEN *[as before]*.   Did you see Bartley?

MAURYA.   I seen the fearfulest thing.

CATHLEEN *[leaves her wheel, and looks out]*, God forgive you; he's riding the mare now over the green head, and the gray pony behind him.

MAURYA *[starts, so that her shawl falls back from her head and shows her white tossed hair. With a frightened voice]*. The gray pony behind him . . .

CATHLEEN *[coming to the fire]*. What is it ails you, at all?

MAURYA *[speaking very slowly]*. . . . I've seen the fearfulest thing any person has seen, since the day Bride Dara saw the dead man with the child in his arms.

CATHLEEN and NORA.   Uali!

[They crouch down in front of the old woman at the fire.]

NORA.   Tell us what it is you seen.

MAURYA. ... I went down to the spring well, and I stood there saying a prayer to myself. Then Bartley came along, and he riding on the red mare with the gray pony behind him *[she puts up her hands, as if to hide something from her eyes]*.   The Son of God spare us, Nora.

CATHLEEN.   What is it you seen?

MAURYA.   I seen Michael himself.

CATHLEEN *[speaking softly]*. You did not, mother; it wasn't Michael you seen, for his body is after being found in the far north, and he's got a clean burial by the grace of God.

MAURYA *[a little defiantly]*. I'm after seeing him this day, and he riding and galloping. Bartley came first on the red mare: and I tried to say 'God speed you,' but something choked the words in my throat. He went by quickly; and 'the blessing of God on you,' says he, and I could say nothing. I looked up then, and I crying, at the gray pony, and there was Michael upon it—with fine clothes on him, and new shoes on his feet.

CATHLEEN *[begins to keen]*. It's destroyed we are from this day. It's destroyed, surely.

NORA. Didn't the young priest say the Almighty God won't leave her destitute with no son living?

MAURYA *[in a low voice but clearly]*. It's a little the like of him knows of the sea.——Bartley will be lost now, and let you call in Eamon and make me a good coffin out of the white boards, for I won't live after them. I've had a husband, and a husband's father, and six sons in this house —six fine men, though it was a hard birth I had with everyone of them and they coming to the world—and there were some of them were found and some of them were not found, but they're gone now the lot of them. There was Stephen and Shawn were lost in the great wind, and found after in the Bay of Gregory of the Golden Mouth, and carried up the two of them on one plank, and in by that door.

[She pauses for a moment; the girls start as if they heard something through the door that is half open behind them.]

NORA *[in a whisper]*. Did you hear that, Cathleen? Did you hear a noise in the North-East?

CATHLEEN *[in a whisper]*. There's some one after crying out by the seashore.

MAURYA *[continues without hearing anything]*. There was Sheamus and his father, and his own father again, were lost in a dark night, and not a stick or a sign was seen of them when the sun went up. . . . There was Patch after was drowned out of a curagh that turned over. I was sitting here with Bartley, and he a baby, lying on my two knees and I saw two women, and three women, and four women coming in, and they crossing themselves, and not saying a word. ... I looked out then, and there were men coming after them, and they holding a thing in the half of a red sail, and water dripping out of it— it was a dry day, Nora— and leaving a track to the door. *[She pauses again with her hand stretched out towards the door. It opens softly and old women*

begin to come in,crossing themselves on the thresh-
old, and kneeling down in front of the stage with
their backs to the people, and the white waist-bands
of the red petticoats they wear over their heads just
seen from behind.]

MAURYA *[half in a dream, to* CATHLEEN]. Is it
Patch, or Michael, or what is it at all?

CATHLEEN. Michael is after being found in the far
north, and when he is found there, how could he be
here in this place?

MAURYA. There does be a power of young men
floating round in the sea, and what way would they
know if it was Michael they had, or another man
like him, for when a man is nine days in the sea,
and a wind blowing, it's hard set his own mother
would be to say what man was in it.

CATHLEEN. It's Michael, God spare him, for
they're after sending us a bit of his clothes from the
far north. *[She reaches out and hands* MAURYA *the
clothes that belonged to* MICHAEL. MAURYA *stands
up slowly, and takes them in her hands. . . .* NORA
looks out.]

NORA. They're carrying a thing among them and
there's water dripping out of it and leaving a track
by the big stones. . . .

CATHLEEN *[in a whisper to the women who have
come in].*   It is Bartley it is?

ONE OF THE WOMEN. . . . It is surely, God rest his
soul.

*[The two younger women come in and pull out
the table. Then men carry in the body of Bartley,
laid on a plank, with a bit of sail over it, and lay it
on the table.]*

CATHLEEN *[to the women, as they are doing so].*
What way was he drowned?

ONE OF THE WOMEN. The gray pony knocked him
over into the sea, and he was washed out where
there is a great surf on the white rocks.

*[*MAURYA *has gone over and knelt down at the
head of the table. The women are keening softly and
swaying themselves with a slow movement.*

CATHLEEN *and* NORA *kneel at the other end oj the table. The men kneel near the door.]*

MAURYA *[raising her head and speaking as if she did not see the people round her].* They're all gone now, and there isn't anything more the sea can do to me . . . I'll have no call now to be up crying and praying when the winds break from the south, and you can hear the surf is in the east, and the surf is in the west, making a great stir with the two noises, and they hitting one on the other. I'll have no call now to be going down and getting Holy Water in the dark nights after Shamhain, and I won't care what way the sea is when the other women will be keening. . . *[To* NORA] . . . Give me the Holy Water, Nora, there's a small sup still on the dresser, [NORA *gives it to her.]*

[MAURYA *drops* MICHAEL'S *clothes across* BARTLEY'S *feet and sprinkles the Holy Water over him].* ... It isn't that I haven't said prayers in the dark night till you wouldn't know what I'd be saying; but it's a great rest I'll have now, and it's time surely. It's a great rest I'll have now, and great sleeping in the long nights after Shamhain, if it's only a bit of wet flour we do have to eat, and maybe a fish that would be stinking. *[She kneels down again, crossing herself, and saying prayers under her breath.]*

CATHLEEN *[to one of the men].* Maybe yourself and Eamon would make a coffin when the sun rises. We have fine white boards herself bought, God help her, thinking Michael would be found, and I have a new cake you can eat while you'll be working.

THE MAN *[looking at the boards].* Are there nails with them?

CATHLEEN. There are not, Colum; we didn't think of the nails.

ANOTHER MAN. It's a great wonder she wouldn't think of the nails, and all the coffins she's seen made already.

CATHLEEN.   It's getting old she is and broken.

[MAURYA *stands up again very slowly and spreads out the pieces of* MICHAEL'S *clothes beside the body, sprinkling them with the last of the Holy Water.*]

NORA [*in a whisper to* CATHLEEN] . She's quiet now and easy; but the day Michael was drowned you could hear her crying out from this to the spring well. It's fonder she was of Michael, and would anyone have thought that?

CATHLEEN [*slowly and clearly*]. An old woman will be soon tired with anything she will do, and isn't it nine days herself is after crying, and keening, and making great sorrow in the house?

MAURYA [*puts the empty cup mouth downward on the table, and lays her hands together on* BARTLEY'S *feet*]. They're all together this time, and the end is come. May the Almighty God have mercy on Bartley's soul, and on Michael's soul, and on the souls of Sheamus, and Patch, and Stephen, and Shawn [*bending her head*], and may He have mercy on my soul, Nora, and on the soul of everyone is left living in the world. [*She pauses, and the keen rises a little more loudly from the women, then sinks away.*]

MAURYA [*continuing*]. Michael has a clean burial in the far north, by the grace of the Almighty God. Bartley will have a fine coffin out of the white boards, and a deep grave surely. What more can we want than that? No man at all can be living forever, and we must be satisfied. [*She kneels down again, and the curtain falls slowly.*]

Made in the USA
Monee, IL
07 July 2026

56552252R00036